THE DREAMER'S HEART

Soulful Poetic Observations of Life

By

Sean Williams

Williams / THE DREAMER'S HEART

Soulful Poetic Observations of Life / 2

<u>INTRODUCTION</u>

Where do I begin? How do I start? I could start from

the very beginning about when I was born and how I

grew up, but that would take too long. This book is not

meant to be a memoir. The whole purpose in why I've

written this book is a journey and collection of

experiences and things that I have seen, and people

encountered, but this is not a biography of my life

story. What I can tell you in this introduction is that I

am a man who has had many battles with depression and still battles it to this very day.

In fact, I have battled it since I was in my teen years. It was just that back then, I did my best to hide it because I made myself believe in two words when I encountered a depression spell: "Suck It Up." I didn't know that things like depression or anxiety or mental illness were even a thing, as I'm sure that a lot of us didn't back then. I stand here today as I write these words to tell you in fact that it is in fact real and the effects can be devastating if you let them take hold of you.

Just so that we're clear, I am by no means a medical expert nor do I pretend to be. For many of us that have battled depression, anxiety or some kind of mental illness, I'm sure those like myself have heard these words a lot. "What do you have to be depressed about?" I grew up in a loving family and I had loving parents that raised me right, but the thing that I've learned is that it doesn't matter if you had a good or bad upbringing. We're all capable of depression manifesting itself in us.

So, what caused depression to become a part of my life? It's a number of things really, things like expectations both educationally and professionally that I didn't think I could live up to, friendships that fell apart, lack of a love life, or comparing myself and where I was at in my life to other people in my life and where they were at in theirs. The unfortunate result of the last one being that it leaves you to believe that somewhere along the way, life left you behind and blessed other people, but forgot you.

When you're battling depression, there will be bad days and they can be bad enough that you'll feel like they'll push you to the edge. Poetry was my coping mechanism, one of many that got me through and helped me along the way and it's my hope that in sharing my words that this will help those that battle depression or anxiety in their life. The words that composite my poems in this book come from my experiences, my dreams, my very soul. What poetry has done for me is help me find even in the blackest of darkness, that one glimmer of light.

These words that are my writings are the words of a soulful dreamer. I share these writings with the dreamers and hopefuls with the hope that they serve to inspire and bestow hope even when you're going through the darkest of times. So, thank you for taking the time in reading my work and my words. My hope is that in sharing these with you, that they will make you smile, feel a sense hope. Poetry was something

that helped find the light in me and I hope that in

sharing my poems, may it help you find yours.

DREAMER'S SONG

I am a Dreamer.

The only drumbeat that I march to is my own.

Being a Dreamer is something to me

Something that I take pride in.

It is not a weakness

It is my strength

It manifests from my heart

From my soul

Being a Dreamer, enables me

Allows me to remember

Remembering to believe

To hope

But also, to remember love

To remember compassion

And in looking back

Remembering the people who I learned it from

We all march to the beat of our own drum

And there is a melody

In the song that is played

The melody in my drumbeat's song

Serves as a reminder:

Defy Expectations

Live for Your Own

Stand Out

Even if you defy the world

Live in yours

Believe in letting things fall

Wherever they may

And that whatever path I choose

Choose the one that makes sense

Even if it doesn't make sense to others

Make sure it makes sense for you

I choose to be a Dreamer

It may not make sense to others

But it does to me

Because I'm always going to be dreaming

Dreaming bigger

Reaching for the stars

Always trying, no matter the falls

Believing in anything being possible

Looking back at years gone past

The song stays the same.

<u>VELOCITY</u>

The superhero that I find myself

Even today as an adult is The Flash

There would be moments where I wondered

What it would feel like

To be known as the fastest man alive

Not just for the ability to go anywhere in the world

Or any point in time

Without limits

But it's also the idea

Of going so fast to the point

That nothing can catch up to you

Nothing can even touch you

Not past mistakes, old regrets,

Or even heartbreaks and losses

The ability to move so fast

You leave it all in the dust.

But the truth is that in life,

It is not about outrunning those moments of the past.

It is about running head on.

To the moments that lie ahead

Always at top speed

Full throttle

Riding that bolt of lighting

We may not have super speed

But when you're charging head on

Right into those moments along the way

You don't have to have super speed

You just run right into them

No regrets

No fear

No hesitation

Just simply run like hell

Maximum velocity within you.

STRENGTH WITHIN

There have been times in life

Where three words at one point or another

Have been often used.

Those three words being from the quote:

"Only the Strong."

While I have applied those words

To the way in which I choose to live,

It is not in terms of physical strength

That I envision those words.

I never consider myself to be a fighter

Or at least to be looking for a fight.

Nor do I believe in pure strength

To come from brute force.

I consider my greatest strength

To be from deep within.

Deep within my mind, my heart

And lastly, my soul.

Remembering those things

In every chance that I can,

Leaves a more empowering feeling

That is indescribable

And immeasurable

It is a strength that can't be duplicated

But it is something that guides me.

Defines myself to my very core.

Helping me to remember always

My beliefs

My honor

And remembering always

Those that matter the most to me.

It is in that regard where I know

My greatest attributes

As well as having a good idea

Both of who I am

And who I want to be.

LITTLE MIRACLE

The day where my life changed forever

Was also the day that this family was blessed.

Everyone talks about the end of one chapter

And the beginning of a new chapter in our lives.

This was the one moment I could remember

Where not only a new chapter began in my life

But that I also felt it begin

All of this took place

On the day that you were born.

The same day that my brother and his wife

Called you their son.

The same day where my parents

Called you their grandson.

And the same day where I looked upon you

And called you my nephew

It was then that I made a vow

That I would want to be the best uncle

That I could possibly be to you.

A vow that I would always,

Always do right by you.

My life has been forever changed

From the moment that you were born.

The moment you entered our lives

A moment that I am now

And forever will be grateful for

That is the birth of you

The little miracle.

<u>HERO</u>

In the beginning of our lives,

We didn't always get along.

There would be a lot of fights.

And more times than not,

Looking back on it now,

They were pretty trivial and stupid

The things that we would fight about.

But as both of us got older,

We bonded along the way

Nobody had my back more times than you did

I was the older one

I was the big brother

And though it was no it was never a contest

You were hands down the better brother.

Because even as we are now

There's nobody I trust more with my life

And one of the few people in my life

That I never want to let down.

That I never want to disappoint.

You been my protector, my friend,

And my greatest hero.

I don't know if I will ever measure up

To be anything close to how you've turned out

I don't know if it's even possible.

But the one thing that drives me

Is the hope that I will never let you down.

Even the words "Thank You" don't seem to say it

enough

To the one who has been my protector,

My brother, My friend

My guardian.

<u>FOUND</u>

There have been five.

Five people in my life

Who have been impactful in it

One of which is family

Two I have known since I was six

One who has been there for me

Even during my darkest moments

To talk me down

And one who is a trusted friend

Whose patience knows no bounds.

What he shares in common with the three others

Who were also described

Is that family isn't always defined

Solely by blood

The other thing these five have in common

With each other

It is because of them that I believe

That love actually does exist

And that in fact can be found

Because the one who is my brother in blood

And the four who are defined to me as family

Have found it for themselves

A long journey

An even longer search

But finding the loves of their lives

It is cause of them that I continue on

To believe in the idea of finding love

Because they did.

<u>IGNITED</u>

There has been my share of heartbreaks

Trusts that were betrayed

I was knocked down

Fallen flat, feeling defeated

Heart shattered on the ground

Been through the pain of heartache

My very being turned to ashes

But in those ashes

A spark ignites

The spark becoming the flame

Expanding like wings of fire

A phoenix rising from the ashes

I've been burnt, but I stand unscathed

The scars of heartache worn

As reminders of lessons learned,

Instead of mistakes to be cursed for.

I may have felt beaten and lost

But there is plenty of fight left in me.

Tears are cast out

Fear thrown to the wayside

Knowing I've gained scars along the way

Taken bumps and bruises

But will not be broken

Will not be playing games

Knowing that I do what I do best

I survive, I fight for my life

Because the hardships along the way

Didn't weaken me.

They made me stronger

And in that strength,

This phoenix will take flight

A fire ignited.

<u>REFLECT</u>

A part of me that wishes

That I could be saying this to your face

Instead of writing these words.

But sometimes in life

That's not how it works

And there's reasons why

Meeting Face to Face shouldn't happen.

I used to tell myself that the reason was because

I could never trust you again.

But truthfully, the one that I don't trust is me.

Because as much as I would say otherwise,

That I would never give you another chance

Or that you've run out of chances,

I'm afraid that somehow, some way,

I would still find myself giving you another chance.

And that does neither of us any good.

Pain and hate can become a curse.

It can even become poisonous.

What happened had to happen

Because you were a lesson that had to be learned

Even if it was learning it the hard way.

There is nothing apologetic about these words

Apologies are moot at this point and serve no

purpose

There is no malicious intent or vengefulness in these

words

No grudge, no spite, no hate

Only thing desired is forgiveness

But you're not the one who forgiveness I seek.

The one whose forgiveness that is long desired

Belongs to the face looking back at me

When I look into the mirror.

Forgiveness for bad judgment

For not trusting my instincts

Not trusting, and ignoring the words of those

Who had my best interests at heart.

Forgiveness for mistakes and accepting that myself

Much like the rest of us are only human.

And part of being human

Finds it easier to forgive an enemy

When they're out of your life.

But forgiving one's self proves to be much harder.

Because while we won't see an enemy again.

Once they've disappeared from our lives

You see yourself everyday

Looking back in the mirror.

Everyday a chance to reflect.

THE WALL

I'm not the one that breaks hearts.

I'm the one who gets his heart broken.

Not the one that leaves anyone behind.

I'm the one who's gotten left behind.

I'm horrible when it comes

to relationships

But I don't want to be.

All those things stare back at me.

Like an impenetrable wall.

Impossible to get around.

Impossible to climb over.

I keep striking at it.

Blow by blow

Strike by strike.

Determined to take that wall down

Piece by piece

I want to tear it to the ground.

However long it takes.

It won't be the wall that stands

It will be me.

SOUNDTRACK

It was on a boulevard of broken dreams

When I came face to face

With the dark shadows of my depression

It was an instant star who sang

About heading for higher ground,

Eagles soared high above,

Spreading the words

That love would keep us alive.

Or a man who sang about love lifting us up

Where we belong

Or telling a girl that it feels like forever.

One band says listen to your heart,

Another talks about when lightning crashes

Songs like these, I hear them.

They illuminate directly to my heart with light.

Awakens a great many things.

Creativity

Kindness

Compassion

Believing in no matter how dark

Or how bleak the darkness

The light always returns

A playlist that is endless, growing every day

The soundtrack of my soul.

FACE-OFF

Since I was in my teenage years

It's stared back at me

Telling me I wasn't good enough

Criticizing my self-worth

Because of expectations that were laid upon me

Telling me I'm a failure because I can't measure up

to them

That the friendships that feel were my own fault

That the betrayals endured were what I deserved

Even as an adult

I'm face to face with it

Every day and every night

I been fighting the darkness that I call my depression

Been fighting it most of my life

No matter how many times I overcome it,

It always returns, it always resurfaces

Coming back ready to tear into me, to tear me down.

Bring me down to my knees

Pushing me to the brink

There are days where I'm poised to fight and ready

And there are days when I feel like the underdog

But that's when I had a theory

That maybe it's not facing off with me to be beaten

Maybe it's facing against me to be fought

And that the game remains unchanged

Digging deep just as before, just as always

To find the will to fight

And eventually finding the will to fight

Never backing down

There is still a breath in me

And in turn, there remains

A lot of fight left in me.

I get back up, staring right back at it

To remind it that of these words, of these vows

That no matter how often you knock me down

I'm always going to get back up, hungry for more

Taking everything you hit me with

Because I have the heart of a fighter

You hold no power over me.

Because your power relies on doubt and on fear

Like a darkness that consumes and corrupts

But it will never consume me and never corrupt me.

Because I will stand back up

I will always stand back up

Staring right back

Saying in all volumes whether it be a whisper,

Or shouting from the mountain tops, or screaming

Right into the heavens above.

Saying to that darkness that you are wrong about me.

That everything you say to me to bring me down

All that you say to hurt me

All that you to do to make me crumble to the ground

I will always say right into your face that you are

wrong about me

And you will ways be wrong.

Because you are nothing but my depression

You exist only in shadows, only in darkness

While this I know true about myself

I believe in the light, I stand in the light

So, go ahead.

Go on, ring the bell

Be ready for a fight

Because I am

And I always will be.

FEARFUL VISION

My greatest fear

A lot of times when I think of the future

It's the one that haunts me the most.

The day where I saw my brother get married

I remember the reception, the dinner

My speech, but also my father's speech to the bride

and groom

I thought to myself how beautiful it was

And how much I wanted those moments for myself.

But as time goes on, nobody at my side

The fear becomes greater with every year

The idea of if that day comes,

Not having the people who matter the most to me

To not have them there on that day

Should I find somebody,

But they're not there to see it

This is a vision that terrifies me

More than anything I could fathom

I would look at it if it came to pass

As my greatest failure

Having that day and none of them

were there to see it

It's a nightmare vision

Unlike any I could ever muster

And haunts me now

Continuing to do so

A nightmare among nightmares.

A DIFFERENT BATTLE

When I think about the future,

There are moments where I think about the time

Where I would become a father

Having a child that I can call my own.

But then I think about what I've gone through with

depression

The really bad days and the times where I felt it

pushing me to the brink

All of the damage that was caused from it

The mental and emotional strain

The feeling of loneliness and the abyss staring back

I ponder what I would do if my child

Whether it be a son or a daughter

If they ended up like me

Having to battle with that.

The thought of it doesn't create fearfulness

It creates determination in myself.

Because if there is one thing that I know in battling

depression

I would never want any child grow up like that.

I would never let my child grow up like that.

Because one of the worst things

that depression does

Is the part when you feel

like you're on your own.

And there is no way and no force

on heaven, hell or earth

Where I would let my child go through that.

It goes way beyond wanting him or her to be better

than me.

It all comes down to making sure that he or she

Would never fight that battle alone

Making sure they know that they're not alone.

An entirely different battlefield.

But when it comes to the stakes on that battlefield

It's one I would charge head on into the heat of it all

In half a heartbeat.

<u>HEART</u>

It's through all the hardships and heartaches

Along the long road of a longer journey

Through all the trials, down every tunnel

That lead me to this moment

Leading me to standing here before you.

A lot of moments where I questioned

If life actually knows what it's doing

The feeling like that has been answered

Gazing at you, holding your hand.

Having faith, trusting in the grand scheme

Are two of the many things that I've learned

Just from having you enter my life.

Looking upon you as I speak these words to you

Trusting that you will hear them

Having faith you believe the source

In which these words are emanating from.

You are my heart

You are my soul

You are home, my world.

And that for as long as the sun rises and falls

For as long as the winds blow through the skies

Or as the waves of the seas

Wash over, touching the shores

I give my heart to you

Telling you how my heart is yours

Now and always

You are the vision of my greatest dreams

A dream that I yearn to become a reality.

LONG ROAD'S JOURNEY

Never seen your face

Nor have I heard your voice

I don't even know your name

What I am certain of

And know in my heart to be true

Is that it has been a long road

A lot of times on that road

The turns have been difficult

Some more than others

A lot of times faced with uncertainty

And a lot of those times anything but easy

No matter the roadblocks

Or the treacherous turns

I know in my heart

And in the very core of my soul

The end of the road is where you'll be

And I know that at that very moment

As long and as winding

As the journey has been

You'll be there

And for every turn and for every obstacle

It will have been worth every second

Because in the long road's journey

Was one that lead me to you.

TRUTH BE TOLD

The truth about the good guys in life.

They have a reputation

To be true, to be loyal

And are never anything more or anything less

Then what you see

But then there's the unspoken truth.

They normally don't have in them

The patience for playing games

Or figuring out signals

Deciphering hidden meanings

Behind the things that are said

Because the good guys are true

And we tend to be straight forward

Truth be told, is that what most girls

Fail to see most of all

Is that the thing about the good guys

Is we don't wait around forever

And by the time it's realized

We're already gone.

<u>THE ONE</u>

A Kiss

A hand joined

Held by another hand

An embrace

A day

A night

One single moment

Just one of these

Can change a single thing

And make it everything

Can make a spark into a flame

A flame into an inferno

Taking two halves

Of what was once broken

And making it into one.

For this one soul

To cherish

To love

To hold the hand of, to hold her in my arms

Giving to her my heart

She is yet to be found

Her face is unknown

And yet I walk constantly seeking

She who is all I seek

All I need,

All that I desire

As you can have your millions of girls out there

Or the plenty of fish in the sea

All I wish is to find her

To find she

Find the one.

DREAMER'S SOUL

Looking back, I remember it all

I remember the feeling of your cheek

As it rested against my hand

I remember the feel of your lips

Both against the palm of my hand

And when they made contact with my own

I remember the beauty and the serenity

And the feeling of pure happiness

In the moment, the very beautiful moment

Where the two of us felt as one

I remember the warmth of your breath

The softness of your voice

And every whisper like a symphony

I even remember the feeling after

Where my eyes opened

And the dream was over

And how it still lingers within me

Remembering even now

How the desire to take the dream

And making it real

Has never been stronger

Call it a memory

Call it a dream

But even a beautiful dream

Can change everything

It can ignite fire

Make the flames grow

And it can guide a dreamer

SHAPING DESTINY

Some say the future is written

Others say that it's not

Sometimes we get a feeling

That we're destined for something

Whether destined for greater

Or destined for the opposite of greatness

Sometimes you have those

That say things such as destiny

Is already written, already in motion

As if it was etched in stone

Believing that free will is an illusion

Without ever considering

Maybe they are wrong

That maybe we're not pre-destined

For one path or the other

That our destined path is yet to be paved

And that maybe

Our destiny is not about a future

That is waiting for us at the end of the tunnel

Waiting for us to claim it

But that the real essence of having a destiny

It's not about finding it

But about shaping it

Creating it.

COURAGE OF THE HEART

The feeling is unfamiliar

A feeling of calm

Feeling of peace

A feeling of serenity

Feeling content

A sense of belonging

As if somehow and some reason

I matter to somebody

And accepted for who I am.

With it, should come a feeling of happiness

And yet what was placed instead

Was a sense of confusion

Because of feeling like I was unsure

Unsure of what my feelings are

And perhaps at the same time

Afraid to face what those feelings are

And in turn cast aside them in fear

But in a moment of clarity

A wake-up call of sorts

Comes the realization

That a lot of the times in life

The things you want the most

Are the things that are worth fighting for

That are worth never giving up

Never backing down

And to never stop fighting

For what your heart desires the most

I no longer fear what could be

Or the statistics of what is nothing more

Than a "what if" outcome

Instead I stand my ground

And face what is ahead

Facing it all head on

Because while I have no certain answer

On what exists, I'm no longer afraid

Because I know more than ever

That what we have

Is something worth fighting for

And something that I will never give up on

Never back down from

So bring the future

Bring the truth

Let the pieces fall where they may.

UNFINISHED LOVE STORY

The song "Love Story" by Taylor Swift

Ringing through my mind

References of Juliet for her Romeo

But then there's my story

My love story as it were

Remains unfinished

Time frame of completion

Remains unknown.

All I know is that this is one prince

One Knight

One Romeo who still remains

Seeking his Juliet

Wealth, Religion, Political Views

Are nowhere in the equation

To know what it's like to be missed

Having one moment

Where one day she is found

Where I can say to her

And only to her these words:

"My heart is and will always belong to you"

To find that one angel

To pledge those words

Give my heart to her

That remains to be my dream

My story

That has only begun to be written

But a happy ending is unreachable

Without the core elements of the love story

For this knight is one who keeps riding

Keeps seeking, looking ahead at the horizon

In hopes that one day, one fine day

Finding the girl

To call his princess.

<u>INVISIBLE</u>

Much like the song

I walk on an empty boulevard of broken dreams

Walking that street I carry with me

A damaged heart

A scarred soul

Love life kept in the dark

By the blackest eclipse

Feeling that the nice guys always finish last

Feeling like I am the personification of that

statement

Seeing those that walk around me

Often times feeling

Like they might as well be walking right through me.

Where I walk, Where I stand

I'm always doing it alone

As a shadow, as a ghost

To even see one I see wish I could be with

Opening my heart to her

Is cast into the abyss

Feeling like nothing short of a pipe dream

Any glimmer of those feelings

Often goes unchecked, and unnoticed

Those feelings within, stay within

Where the only one who feels them

Or knows that they exist is me

While to the rest of the world

Those feelings are just the same

As how I feel viewed to the world

As invisible as I am.

<u>FROZEN NATURE</u>

Some call a cold heart a frozen heart

Some go as far as to say about it

That a frozen heart is a heart that cannot feel

Perhaps it is not so much

An inability to feel

But a decision to not want to feel

A matter of choice

Sometimes a matter of pride

Or a matter of self-preservation

A form of protection

In becoming frozen, a wall takes shape

Surrounding the heart in question.

With the sole purpose of being impenetrable

But in that regard it fails to do so

For it is impenetrable only from without

But never from within

Often times, the one with said frozen heart

Will have the desire to break down the walls

Some even choose to fulfill that desire

Once again, it's a matter of choice

Those that have the desire that fail to do so

Do not act because of fear

Or because of seeking a reason to act

And being unsuccessful in finding one

Some would say that having a frozen heart

Or appearing to do so is human nature

But it is also human nature

To break the ice that surrounds

ODE TO AN ANGEL

Whenever I look into your eyes

I feel myself get lost in them

Whenever you smile

I can't help but do the same

To hear your voice calling my name

It sounds sweeter than any music on the planet

Most guys in this world will always dream

Of going all the way with the girl of their dreams

Yet that is a desire that never enters my thoughts

The greatest fantasy for me that I have now

And that I always have had to this day

Is to hold you in my arms

Just so that I would know what it would feel like

To hear your voice whisper my name in my ear

No sound surrounding either of us

It is calm and peaceful

A complete state of serenity around us both

To think of you is like a blessing from heaven

To see you smile is a gift from the gods

Because anytime that I think of you

It's the only time at any point and time in my life

Where I feel as though I can fly to the skies above

Without a care in the world

Or anything around me

Just knowing you alone is the one sense

That I've felt in my life.

Of what strength which generates from my heart

And even in the roots of my very soul itself

And it's a feeling that I feel that words

Can never describe with the justice deserved

Just knowing you alone is the closest thing

To being in an angel's embrace.

<u>HONOR</u>

We often see it in movies

Seen it on TV

Even read about it in stories

About those that believe

Those that follow their lives

In some shape or form,

A code of honor

The word itself can be viewed in different ways

And at the same exact time

Can hold a different purpose

A purpose to inspire

To motivate

To bestow courage

For those that either need more of it

Or those that are without it at all

But for the most part with honor

It gives reason to fight

Stand for what we believe in

What we desire

And of course, to cherish those

That we hold most dear in our hearts

Whether it be for friends

For family or the one in which

Holds our heart to their own

As a token of love exchanged

As a symbolic and honorable bond

In the end, in the darker times

Where we find ourselves

Pushed toward the brink of the abyss

It is both love and honor

That often are the things that keep us

From going over the edge

For it is those two things that bind to us all

And remind us of all that we hold dear

DESIRED REFLECTION

I look to you

The effect of your smile

Always makes me smile

When I'm feeling low

You reach down to pull me up

When darkness feels like it surrounds me

You bring forth the light

I say you make me

You make me want to be a better person

But you tell me there's no need

You tell me that I don't need to be

When I already am

Because you would rather I be just as I am

Nothing more and nothing less

And in turn when I see you

I desire the same of you

For in my eyes, you are perfect

Just the way that you are

Because you represent in my eyes

Everything that is right and good

In what the world should be

But you are also the vision

The desired reflection

Of the kind of person

That I want to strive to be.

<u>INFINITE PRIDE</u>

No Regrets

No Looking Back

No Turning Back

Never changing for anyone else

Other than one's own self

Walking tall,

Standing strong

Always believing

Always dreaming

I may be judged by others

For talking the way that I do

With a voice sounding too deep

For not being the most physically built

Or even being the tallest person

I may be judged for the tastes and interests

That I have in movies, music or TV.

All of this may be true.

For I am not the tallest or the most muscular

And I have varied interests

In the TV and movies that I choose to watch

And even the music that I choose to listen to

But nobody is better than me

No matter how much of me is pointed out

Or how much is targeted for criticism

The person that stands here now

Is the person that I am most proud to be

For I would rather live my life

Being the person that I am

Then spend my life

Pretending to be something that I'm not

Because for anyone who deals with this

The difference between ourselves

And those that criticize

Is that in accepting ourselves

For the people that we are

We find that our own opinion

Is all that matters

Once that infinite supply

Of our own pride in one's self

Is brought into the light.

THE FRIEND

It feels like so long ago

When you and I met

A friendship was formed

No matter how bad things got for me

Or how much all the anxiety

All the depression got the better of me

You were always there

Always there to throw the life preserver

To reel me back to safety

Refusing to ever let it get the better of me

You were the safety net

Always there to grab my hand

When I felt like I was falling

Your grip never loosening for even a second

While it feels like forever

Since the day that this friendship began

You never stopped being there

Sending cards for no reason at all

Except for the reason to make sure I knew

How loved that I am

How much the friendship you and I have is valued

You watch over me like a watchful guardian

Even go as far as to say a guardian angel

I know for certain how fortunate I am to know you

But I also can't begin to imagine

The kind of person I would have ended up

If I hadn't met you

Frankly, I am not sure if I even want to.

I just know that there is no gift

that I could ask for in my life

Then having the honor of knowing you.

EPILOGUE &

ACKNOWLEDGMENTS

There are a lot of people that I want to be able to thank for being a huge part of my life and that in turn inspired me to find my voice. My parents Kevin and Joanne who raised me. My brother Daniel who has always had my back as well as his wife Hilda who have the most amazing child that I have the honor to be his uncle. My friends Trevor and Tyler along with their wives Crystal and Katie who have the most amazing girls that I am also privileged and honored to have them also call me an uncle.

My friend Matt and his wife Jenna who without question has got to be one of the most patient people that I know, I know that I'm grateful in the fact that he and Jenna have found each other and are still married even at the time of writing this. Most of all I want to also thank my friend Kelly who has been my guiding light

and always saw the best in me and strived with

all her heart to help me see what she sees with me

everyday and that her friendship I couldn't be

more thankful for having.

I also want to acknowledge bands like

Green Day and Linkin Park and of course singer

and actress from the show "Instant Star" Alexz

Johnson who all their music helped to inspire

me and got me through some difficult times

while I battled with my anxiety and my

depression. There have also been some people

in my life who I have gotten burned by along the

way, but while I won't acknowledge them by

name, I do thank them for the fact that I became

a stronger person because of them and that they

were lessons in my life that I had to learn and

for that I thank them for it.

I also want to acknowledge TV shows like
Make It Or Break It, Arrow, The Flash, Supergirl,
The Vampire Diaries, The Originals and
Legacies along with the Marvel Cinematic
Universe movies. It was from watching these
that not only got me through my depression by
giving me an escape from reality, but also
inspired me to reach higher and find something
greater than I believed to be possible.

And lastly, to those that have bought this

book, I want to thank you for purchasing this

book whether it be that you downloaded it as a

kindle book or bought it as a paperback for

following me in my words written in my poems

in this book. This has been my first venture into

writing a book and even as I write this, I find

myself in awe at the fact that it is done and that

many people like yourselves will be able to read

my work.

I'm hoping that for those who read this and

that may have battled anxiety or depression

somewhere along the way or even do so now,

that maybe this will help you along whatever

path you follow in your life in just knowing that

you are not alone and that we all have the

ability to find a light and find our voice that will

guide us through it all. This book and writing

poetry have been how I was able to find my

light and my voice. My hope is that those that

find hope or find some kind inspiration from

my words, will find their voice and find their

light in some shape or form.

From the bottom of my soul, thank you

for reading this book and taking this journey

through this dreamer's heart.

Soulful Poetic Observations of Life / 127

Soulful Poetic Observations of Life / 130